Open the Meeting
with Prayer

OPEN
THE MEETING
WITH PRAYER

Revised by Harry N. Huxhold

Publishing House
St. Louis   London

Concordia Publishing House, St. Louis, Missouri
Concordia Publishing House Ltd., London E.C.1
Copyright © 1973 Concordia Publishing House
Library of Congress Catalog Card No. 55-7442
International Standard Book No. 0-570-03147-8

Contents

Preface

THIS LITTLE VOLUME was originally prepared chiefly for the layman who is called on to open a meeting with prayer. Alfred Doerffler was the editor, of the first edition, which ran through several printings. Sixty-five pastors, teachers, professors, and church administrators contributed prayers from the richness of their experiences.

The present edition updates some of the language that has become archaic in less than one generation of our age of change. Prayers have been added for the benefit of some church groups that meet frequently. Prayers have been written also for some groups that were not represented in the first edition.

May these prayers invoke much grace and blessings for all who use them to open the meeting with prayer.

Harry N. Huxhold

An Order for the Opening of a Meeting

The meeting may begin with one of the appropriate prayers. If a longer opening is desired, the following order may be used:

A hymn may be sung or read.

Leader: In the name of the Father and of the Son and of the Holy Spirit.

All: **Amen.**

A psalm or lesson may be read by the leader.

After the reading of a psalm all say:
Glory be to the Father and to the Son and to the Holy Spirit; as it was in the beginning, is now, and ever shall be, world without end. Amen.

APPROPRIATE HYMNS:
Holy Ghost, with Light Divine

God Himself Is Present
This Is the Day the Lord Hath Made
Renew Me, O Eternal Light
Let Us Ever Walk with Jesus
May We Thy Precepts, Lord, Fulfil

APPROPRIATE PSALMS OR LESSONS:

Psalm 1	Matthew 5:11-16
Psalm 8	Matthew 11:25-30
Psalm 24	Matthew 20:20-28
Psalm 46	Luke 14:25-35
Psalm 67	Luke 17:5-10
Psalm 100	John 3:31-36
Psalm 121	John 4:31-38
Psalm 122	Acts 14:21-28
Psalm 127	1 Corinthians 12:4-13
Psalm 133	2 Corinthians 4:1-6
Psalm 134	Ephesians 1:15-23
Psalm 150	Philippians 1:3-11

An Order for the Closing of a Meeting

The leader may close with one of the appropriate benedictions. If a longer closing is desired, the following order may be used:

> *A hymn may be sung or read.*
>
> *All may say the Apostles' Creed.*
> or
> *All may say the Lord's Prayer.*
>
> *The·leader may say an appropriate benediction.*
> *All say:* **Amen.**
> or
> *The leader may say: Bless we the Lord.*
> *All say:* **Thanks be to God.**

APPROPRIATE HYMNS:
> The Common Doxology
> Lord, Dismiss Us with Thy Blessing

Now May He Who from the Dead
Abide, O Dearest Jesus
Guide Me, O Thou Great Jehovah

APPROPRIATE BENEDICTIONS:
Unto Him who is able to do exceeding abundantly above all that we ask or think according to the power that works in us, unto Him be glory in the church and in Christ Jesus throughout all ages, world without end. Amen.

May the blessing of God Almighty, the Father, the Son, and the Holy Spirit, rest on us and on all our work and worship done in His name. May He give us His light to guide us, His Spirit to encourage us, and His love to unite us now and forever. Amen.

Unto the King, eternal, immortal, invisible, the only wise God, be honor and glory forever and ever. Amen.

The almighty God, the Father of our Lord Jesus Christ, of whom the whole family in heaven and earth is named, grant us to be strengthened with might by His Spirit in the inner man, that, Christ dwelling in our hearts by faith, we may be filled with all the fullness of God. Amen.

Altar Guild

1

O ETERNAL GOD, You have given to Your church many precious gifts, brought us into Your Kingdom by the means of grace, and blessed our work through the power of the Holy Spirit. We thank You for the opportunities to serve as helpers in Christ Jesus. May we, like the pious women of old, serve You with a humble and quiet spirit, that our labors may be blessed to the glory of Your name. As You have appointed women to care for Your sanctuary, kindle in our hearts the fire of faith and love of Your house to give Your altar reverent attention. May we never grow weary in well-doing, but continue to treasure every opportunity to be kind to the poor, hospitable to Your saints, and generous in our charities, until that great day when our worship and service will be perfected before Your eternal throne of grace in life everlasting, through the merits of Jesus Christ, our Savior. Amen.

2

LORD JESUS, OUR BLESSED SAVIOR, in whose presence real joy may be found, grant that we may find our highest good in Your service. Let the faithful women who were last at Your cross and first at Your tomb be our examples. Like Mary, may we give attention to the one thing needful, refusing to be distracted by the clamor and tension of life. Let us learn at Your feet those things that make us wise unto salvation. Come into our hearts, which are kept as quiet chambers for You. Adorn us with beauty of spirit that our hearts may be set not on outward things but on good works that please You and benefit our fellowmen. Grant that we may treasure spiritual riches above the price of precious jewels, for favor often is deceitful and beauty is passing, but wisdom and virtue are crowns of great worth. Increase among us the spirit of peace and mutual understanding that we may fulfill our high calling in Christ Jesus, to the praise of Your most holy name. Amen.

3

MOST GRACIOUS FATHER IN HEAVEN, because You bless our sanctuary on earth with Your heavenly presence in Word and sacraments, we devoutly gather to worship You. Lord, we love the habitation of Your house and the place where Your honor dwells. By Your grace enable us to render quality service to You in our care of the sacred appointments, vestments, and vessels of Your house. Help us that our worship of You may be enhanced, our services beautified, and all things we do in Your name may be glorified. Accept the service of our hands we give lovingly to You. Grant us and all who worship You here true love for You, for Your house, and for Your Word. In the name of Jesus Christ, our Savior. Amen.

4

HEAVENLY FATHER, whom to know is to love and whom to love is to serve, grant us Your abiding presence in our meeting and Your blessings on our consecrated service. Cleanse our thoughts and the desires of our hearts that we may perfectly love You and honestly serve You in faith. Grant us the spirit of reverence and devotion that all things may be done reverently and in order in the care of Your sanctuary, in the dressing of Your altar, in the care and preparation of the sacred vessels, and in all other duties entrusted to our guild. Then will our sacrifice of service be acceptable to You and our good works magnify Your most holy name. In the name of Christ, our Lord. Amen.

incarnate in Your Son Jesus; and as Your Word was preserved for us by Spirit-filled prophets, evangelists, and apostles; give us Your Holy Spirit that Your Word may become incarnate again in our lives through Him who is our Redeemer and King. Amen.

Bible Class (Studying the Old Testament)

LORD GOD OF ABRAHAM, ISAAC, AND JACOB, as You guided the host of Israel from Egyptian slavery to the Land of Promise, lead us now from captivity of our ignorance into the promises of Your Word. As the cloud of smoke and pillar of fire marked Israel's path in the desert of wandering, let Your Spirit accompany us as we move in the pages of Your Book. Let there be no darkness on our way. Let Your fatherly benediction, the love of Your Son Jesus Christ, and the inspiration of Your Spirit illumine us even as He illumined Moses and Joshua of old. Open Your Word to us. Speak clearly and warmly to us, who are heirs with Christ of the Land of Promise, even our home in heaven. We ask this in His name, the Messiah foretold and crucified and risen—for us. Amen.

Bible Class
(Studying the New
Testament)

SAVIOR OF MANKIND, whose cradle forever is the Gospel of salvation, we pray You to give us the grace to take You from that cradle into the recesses of our hearts. Let our study of the Bible reveal to us the fullness of Your redeeming love—in Your birth, life, death, and resurrection. May Your Word never find us without inquisitive eyes, reaching hands, and restless feet. Let Your words take life before our eyes that we may be warmed by Your very presence. Live in us, Lord Jesus. Work in us. And let the Book, which as a cradle holds You before us, enjoy reverence, regular reading, and study among us. In Your own name we pray. Amen.

Board of Directors or Trustees

1

LORD JESUS CHRIST, as You sit on the right hand of God the Father Almighty to rule and govern Your church, we acknowledge You as our Prophet, Priest, and King. Bless the prophetic Word that is preached and taught in our church, that Your people may be edified by it. Impress on our members at all times their calling to the royal priesthood. Rule over our congregation as our King, and guide us in all things. Grant that what we consider and resolve in this meeting will be to Your glory and for the welfare of our church. Lord Jesus, our Savior, we commend ourselves to You and our congregation to Your care. Permit us to attend to the tasks of Your kingdom in the assurance that You are with us. Amen.

2

LORD JESUS CHRIST, as You give to Your church the authority to choose deacons for the many tasks in a Christian congregation, bless us with wisdom, patience, and piety to carry out our obligations and duties. Preserve a harmonious spirit among us, a spirit of wisdom and understanding, so that we maintain unity of action. May we inspire our members to support generously the needs and maintenance of the church and the building of Your church at large, its missions and charities at home and abroad. Give us Your Holy Spirit, that we may carry out our duties and exercise the authority given us by this congregation in full agreement and with due observance of Your holy Word. Amen.

3

LORD OF THE CHURCH AND OUR SAVIOR, we invite Your presence as we discuss the business of Your church, which You have purchased with Your lifeblood. As You have made us responsible for the welfare of the flock of Christ at this place, grant us the wisdom and understanding which come from above. Enable us to know those things that You will have us do so that Your kingdom may be advanced among us. Give us the willingness to spend and be spent in laboring for You. May we count no cost too great, no labor too exhausting, and no goal too high in striving to do Your holy will. Use our time, talents, and treasury in doing Your work while it is still day, before the night comes when no man can work. Hear our prayer and grant it for Your own sake. Amen.

4

LORD JESUS CHRIST, Head and Bishop of the church, we offer You the praise of our lips and the gratitude of our hearts for the many evidences of Your goodness to us. We thank You that You have called us out of spiritual darkness into the marvelous light of Your Gospel. We praise You that You have established Your church among us and have given us the high privilege and honor of being leaders in this congregation. We confess that without You we can do nothing. Therefore, we ask Your guidance as we seek to carry out the responsibility of leadership committed to us. Direct our thoughts to make whatever we do pleasing to You. Help us always to promote the interest of Your kingdom. Prosper the work that we undertake to Your glory and for the salvation of many precious, blood-bought souls. All this we ask confidently and courageously in Your name. Amen.

Board of Education

1

O ALMIGHTY GOD, HEAVENLY FATHER, Giver of all that is good, without whose help all labor is ineffectual and without whose grace all wisdom falters, we come before You with a deep sense that we are inadequate to perform our work as leaders and teachers in the Christian training of the members of our church, who have been redeemed with the precious blood of Your dear Son. We pray that You give us the wisdom and strength, the powers and abilities, and the earnestness and consecration we need, so that our guidance and teaching will reflect the glory of Your holy name and serve the temporal and eternal welfare of all who have been entrusted to our care. We ask this for Jesus' sake. Amen.

2

LORD GOD, HEAVENLY FATHER, we thank You for the opportunity to plan and work for the spiritual growth of believers. Fill our hearts with love for You and with the desire to grow in grace and in the knowledge of our Lord and Savior Jesus Christ. Open our hearts and minds that we may see how to help others grow through the study of Your Word. Bless the instruction of the children in our (school and) Sunday school, and give them grace to believe Your Word and to serve You with grateful hearts. Increase the devotion of our young people, of the members of the adult Bible classes, and all our agencies of Christian education. Give to all teachers in the congregation the zeal that is necessary for joyful and successful teaching. Help our congregation to see its mission opportunities ever more clearly, and bless our neighborhood mission efforts. We pray through Jesus Christ, our Lord. Amen.

3

HEAVENLY FATHER, we pray for all the educational agencies of our congregation. May all who teach here be taught by You. May all who learn be guided by Your Holy Spirit. Enable us

27

who plan and administer programs for teachers and students to be instructed by Your heavenly wisdom, through Jesus Christ, our Lord. Amen.

4

GRACIOUS GOD, as You taught Your ancient people Israel through prophets, priests, seers, rabbis, and scribes; and as You gave us the clearest revelation in the Master Teacher Jesus and His apostles and evangelists; by Your Holy Spirit enable us to create, administer, and provide quality educational programs, agencies, and tools that will serve the glory of Your name and the welfare of this congregation for the sake of Christ, our Lord. Amen.

Cemetery Association

1

LORD JESUS, VICTOR OVER DEATH, we know and believe that You are the Resurrection and the Life and that whoever believes in You shall live though he were dead. Enable us to care for our cemetery as the last resting place for the mortal remains of our loved ones now fallen asleep in You. By Your abode in the tomb in Joseph's garden You have hallowed the graves of our cemetery. May our beloved dead rest in the sunshine of Your resurrection. Deepen in us the awareness of our freedom which You won for us by Your death and that we may serve You in joy. As we meet to discuss ways and means of improving, beautifying, and perpetuating this sacred spot in the City of the Dead, we beseech You to grant us an abundant measure of Your Holy Spirit, that He may guide and direct us in our deliberations

31

so that all that we may say, do, and resolve will redound to Your glory. We ask it in Your name, Lord Jesus. Amen.

2

LORD GOD, HEAVENLY FATHER, by Your Son's rest in the tomb You have sanctified the graves of Your saints who lie buried in our cemetery. Hold Your protecting hand over the graves of our loved ones, so that their mortal remains may rest in peace until You call them back into life on the Day of Judgment. Prevent catastrophies and disasters that would disturb their graves. Grant us wisdom and understanding to govern this cemetery, which we hold sacred, for the blessing of all who share with us the hope of life eternal. We ask it for Jesus' sake, who is the Resurrection and the Life. Amen.

Charity Association

1

OUR HEAVENLY FATHER, we bless You because
You have redeemed us from all sin, from death,
and from the power of the devil by Your Son,
our Lord Jesus Christ. We praise You that
You have blessed us richly with all temporal
and eternal blessings. We thank You that by
Your Holy Spirit You have called us by the
holy Gospel to faith and by His power enlightened our eyes. Forgive us our many faults,
our shortcomings, and our sins. Pardon our
hardness of heart, our indifference toward
those in need, our selfishness, and our greed.
Enable us to see the multitude of the sick and
the suffering, the needy and the forsaken with
the eyes of Him who went about doing good to
men. Grant that we may devote our lives, our
strength, our time, our talents, and our means
more fully to Your service. Help us to minister

33

to our needy and suffering fellowmen in Your name, that Your glory may be revealed and Your works be made manifest among all men, through Jesus Christ, our Lord. Amen.

2

O GOD, OUR FATHER, we bless You because You have loved us with an everlasting love revealed through Your Son, our Lord and Savior Jesus Christ. We thank You that You have graciously called us through faith into the fellowship of Your children. We thank You that You have given us Your word to guide us in lives of service to You and our fellowmen. You have given us the commandments to love one another and to bear one another's burdens. We confess that too often we have not remembered these commandments, and we have sinned against You through our indifference toward the needs of our brethren. Forgive us our sins for Jesus' sake. Grant that we may more faithfully serve You in our needy and suffering fellowmen. Have mercy on all who are forsaken and forlorn. May our love for them reflect that saving love with which You have loved us in Christ Jesus. Attend our meetings as we plan this work together, and grant us Your Holy Spirit's power, that we may always do according to Your will and to the honor and glory of Your name, through Jesus Christ, our Lord. Amen.

Choir

1

LORD GOD, HEAVENLY FATHER, in You we live and move and have our being, and from You is all that we possess. Help us by Your Spirit to use all that we are and have to Your praise and glory. May also our service as members of the choir of our congregation find favor in Your sight. Keep our choir free from jealousy and selfishness. Help us to "love one another with brotherly affection, to outdo one another in showing honor." Let the Word of Christ dwell richly in the members of our choir that we may sing with grace in our hearts of Your glory, our Lord and God. In Jesus' name. Amen.

2

HEAVENLY FATHER, we thank You for Your loving-kindness and tender mercy which surrounded us this day and kept us from harm and danger. Help us by Your spirit to live ever closer to You that all we do and say may be directed by Your holy will. Fill our hearts with gratitude for the many blessings we have received from Your bountiful goodness, especially for the forgiveness of our sins for the sake of Jesus Christ, our Savior. And now help us joyfully to prepare to use the gift of song to Your glory. Amen.

3

GRACIOUS FATHER, we thank and praise You that You have given us the reason to bless and glorify You and have put a new song in our hearts through our Lord Jesus Christ. For His sake inspire us to sing with joy and the best that is in us that Your name be hallowed by our service. Amen.

4

BLESSED LORD, we honor You and adore You because You have put melody in our hearts through the redeeming love of Your Son Jesus, and we pray that our hymns and spiritual songs may blend with the choirs of heaven to give endless praise to Him who is our Lord and Savior. Amen.

Congregational Meeting or Voters Assembly

1

HEAVENLY FATHER, whose we are and whom we serve, we give You thanks for life eternal that is ours because we know You as our true God and Father and Jesus Christ as our Redeemer and Lord. Make us ever more zealous in Your service through the power of Your indwelling Spirit. Guide and keep, strengthen and cheer us in all we undertake for You. Sit with us. Give us Your counsel. Help us with the tasks assigned to us. Direct our plans for the advancement of Your work, so that in all things Your name be glorified through Jesus Christ, our Lord. We know You will hear our prayer, dear Father, and grant us Your Holy Spirit for Jesus' sake, in whose name we bring to You our petitions. Amen.

2

Lord God, heavenly Father, whose mercies are new every morning and whose compassions fail not, we give You humble thanks for redeeming us through the death of Your Son, for bringing us to the knowledge of salvation, and for making us members of Your holy church. Since it is Your will that the work of Your church be performed by weak human beings, we beseech You to grant us forgiveness for sins of the past. Be present today in our midst with Your grace and Spirit. Open our eyes to the needs of the church at home and abroad. Furnish us with wisdom and zeal to take the necessary steps to meet those needs. Give us all a humble, peaceable disposition and willingness to do only such things as will redound to Your glory and to the welfare of Your church. We ask it in Jesus' name. Amen.

3

Jesus, we thank You for inviting us to become partners with You in Your Father's business — our Father's business. Help us to be as interested, as diligent, as devoted, as prudent, as courageous in our Father's business as we are in our private undertakings. Let the indwelling of Your Holy Spirit supply those qualities that we lack and are needed especially in our Father's business: brotherly love, a passion for souls, the genius to see opportunities and to make the most of them, a willingness to let Your Word decide every issue, the gift to enlist the cooperation of all members of the congregation. Guide, direct, and give success to our deliberations and decisions. Supply a rich measure of grace to us and others, so that our words and actions may contribute much to the expansion of the Father's business and to the salvation of many. Amen.

4

LORD OF THE CHURCH, because You work through us, we pray You to come into our midst. Enter our innermost selves. Possess us and use us as You will. Have pity on our narrowness, and grant us the vision of a wide world of men whom You would draw to Yourself. Melt our coldness, and make our hearts beat with Your compassion for the erring, the fallen, and the needy both within and outside the church. Shame our idleness, and save us from the sin of complacency and "ease in Zion." Make us willing to spend and be spent for Your kingdom. Let Your kingdom come to us. Prosper Your work in our hands, and let us know the joy of being used for a great cause by a greater Savior. Amen.

5

DEAR LORD JESUS, we meet in Your name. We claim Your gracious promise: "Where two or three are gathered together in My name, there I am in the midst of them." Make Your presence and grace manifest in this meeting. Teach us more and more to appreciate the truth of Your Word as it is proclaimed and taught in Your church and also to make faithful use of Your holy sacraments for the nourishment and enrichment of our spiritual life. Make us eager workers together with You in the building of Your kingdom of grace. Bless us with unity of the spirit. Forgive us when we have come short, and cause us to grow in knowledge and faith, in grace and wisdom. Grant that we may find joy in Your service and gladly give regularly and proportionately of our earthly substance and make the best use of our talents and opportunities. Warm our hearts with love for You, for one another, and especially for those in need or sorrow. Strengthen, guide, and bless our pastor in his sacred and arduous calling. Bless the teachers in our schools, and all others who are associated with the work of our church, that Your name be hallowed, Your kingdom come, and Your will be done among us. Amen.

6

GRACIOUS GOD, OUR HEAVENLY FATHER, we thank You for Your loving kindness, faithfulness, and truth. We praise You because You have made us Your own through the redemption that is in Christ Jesus. We bless You because You have brought us into Your church to daily enrich us with the priceless treasures of Your life-giving and life-sustaining Gospel. Day by day increase in us the appreciation of Your gracious goodness. Consecrate us and all we possess to the glory of Your saving name. Enable us to be active and faithful members of Your church. Grant that our example may be wholesome and helpful to others. Fill our hearts with a fervent desire and a determined purpose to share the blessings of the Gospel with our fellowmen at home and abroad. Equip us for all our responsibilities in church and home. Give Your heavenly benediction to this assembly. Be present with Your Holy Spirit. Let Your Word guide our deliberations and actions, that Your name be glorified and the best interests of the church served. Give us vision and courage to attempt great things for You. We offer our prayer in the name of Christ, our Savior and King. Amen.

Elders

1

O LORD JESUS, OUR SAVIOR, we bless You because You have purchased us with Your blood and by Your grace made us worthy to serve You in our congregation as elders. Keep us and our congregation in peace and harmony in one mind, striving together for the cause of the Gospel. Let Your Word have free course among us. Restore the erring. Strengthen those who are tempted. Comfort the distressed, the sick, and the bereaved. Be present in our deliberations. Guide us by Your Holy Spirit that we may do Your will. Grant us wisdom to resolve the matters You have placed into our hands. Give us courage and perseverance to carry out such resolutions as will redound to Your glory and to the welfare of Your kingdom. Amen.

2

WE THANK YOU, OUR HEAVENLY FATHER, for
having called us into the work of Your church
as elders in our congregation. Help us to remember the ways of Your mercy which bind
us to You in the covenant of Holy Baptism.
Keep us growing in grace and in the knowledge
of our Lord and Savior Jesus Christ. May no
place on earth ever be dearer to us than Your
house and no task more holy than that which
brings souls to repentance and faith. Help
us remember the great men who have been the
leaders of Your church in every age. Give us
grace to recognize that our called pastors and
we are co-workers with You. Give us courage
to serve in these troubled times. Unite our
hearts with You that we may in true harmony
do Your will and be true and worthy servants
of our only Master, even Jesus Christ, Your
Son, our Lord. We ask it in His name and for
His sake. Amen.

3

MERCIFUL AND GRACIOUS FATHER IN HEAVEN,
we thank You for saving us through Christ

that we may glorify You through service. We earnestly ask You to give us humility that we may approach the greatest and the least of our members in an acceptable spirit. Grant us a clear understanding of Your Word that we may apply it effectively as a power to salvation and as a shield and weapon against all forces that would destroy us and our fellow Christians. Accompany, encourage, and guide us as we go out to comfort the sick, strengthen the weak, and recall the straying. Prepare the hearts of those we visit that they may receive us as the servants of Your Son, our Savior, in whose name we pray. Amen.

4

LORD JESUS, as servants of Your kingdom we implore Your Spirit's blessing on our deliberations. Without Your Spirit we can do nothing worthy of Your glory. Therefore we turn to Your counsel and guidance that we may be fully instructed and enlightened by Your Word. May each of us strive to understand Your will. Give us the power to do Your will. May each member of our congregation accept his calling to serve Your kingdom in our midst. Deliver us from the sins of unfaith, disobedience, and indifference. May all of us feel deeply responsible and accountable to You as stewards of the talents You have given us. Finally, bless our resolves that they contribute to Your glory, for Your mercy and for Your truth's sake. Amen.

Evangelism Committee

1

LORD GOD, HEAVENLY FATHER, we thank and praise You that You have called us into the fellowship of saints. Deepen our gratitude for the salvation You have granted us in Your Son, our Lord. Embolden us to be witnesses to His love to all men everywhere. Open the hearts of our fellowmen to the Gospel of Your grace that they may be incorporated with us in the body of Christ, for whose sake we pray it. Amen.

2

GRACIOUS FATHER, we bless You for ordaining that Your Son should redeem the world. Use us for getting the Word of salvation out to those who sit in darkness. Prepare the way for rapid

49

distribution of tracts, gospels, and communications of every sort that will warm men's hearts. Stir Christians everywhere to be ready to give an account of their faith to all men. Gather all the resources necessary for facilitating the cause of the Gospel. Open the hearts and ears of those who stubbornly refuse to hear and believe. Bring witnesses to those who are eager and waiting for Him who can come only as we send and bring His Word. For His sake we pray. Amen.

3

O GOD, OUR HEAVENLY FATHER, we thank You for the gift of Your dear Son. Grant that we who have received Him in our hearts may joyfully go forth in His name to proclaim His peace to others. Bless our efforts in speaking, our ability to understand others, our capacity to love others, our patience in dealing with others, and our willingness to speak the Gospel to all men. Open the hearts of others that they may receive the Good News we bring from our blessed Lord Jesus Christ. Hear us for His sake, Amen.

Finance Committee

1

GRACIOUS HEAVENLY FATHER, we confess that You are a God of power and order, continually preserving the earth and its fullness for our use. Teach us to remember You as our Creator, to glorify You with our reasonable service, and to honor You with our firstfruits. May we remember that You have sent Your Son to make us children of Your grace. Bless our plans for a systematic gathering of offerings and a careful accounting of our stewardship. Pour out Your continual blessing on our congregation that each of us may do his fair share to preach, teach, reach, live, and give for You. We trust Your promises for such blessings, for You have proved Your love for us in Christ Jesus, our Savior, in whose name we pray. Amen.

2

TRULY, O GOD, You are the Giver of every good and perfect gift. Of ourselves we are spiritually poor and barren. Through the poverty and suffering of Your only Son and the sanctifying operation of Your Holy Spirit You make us rich in spirit and fruitful in life. As You continually give us the power to get wealth, so give us the wisdom to plan its wise expenditure. Make us and all members of our congregation good stewards of our earthly treasures that we and many others may enjoy Your heavenly treasures. Give us a healthy national economy that we may labor and have to give to You willingly, cheerfully, and regularly. Lift our eyes to the fields white already to the harvest, and fill our hearts with love to send reapers to the uttermost parts of the earth. Let Your blessing rest on our plans, for without You we can do nothing. Hear us for Jesus' sake. Amen.

3

O LORD JESUS CHRIST, as You once sat at the treasury in the temple to observe how Your people gave, watch over our stewardship efforts now. Grant Your people the willingness and love of the poor widow who gave all that she had. Grant unto us, to whom the care of Your treasury is given, a proper concern like Your own. Enable Your children to give as You have prospered them that Your coffers may be filled with the means to spread the Gospel in the world, to maintain the ordinances of Your house among us, and to provide the means to relieve the sufferings of the sick, the poor, and the aged. We pray in Your name and for Your sake. Amen.

4

O LORD GOD, OUR HEAVENLY FATHER, whose name is Love and whose delight is to manifest Yourself to us as the divine Giver of all good things for this life and for that which is to come, You have given us life and breath and all things needful to sustain us. We thank and praise You for all Your gifts, and especially for the gift of Your Son, who died for us and rose again. Grant Your people to understand ever more deeply the wonders of Your infinite love. Sanctify them by the Gospel of Your love. Let them give themselves to You that they may become ever more like Him, even our Lord Jesus, who, though He was rich, yet for our sakes became poor, that we through His poverty might become rich. In His name we pray. Amen.

Human Relations Society

1

CREATOR GOD, because You have made all nations and kindreds and tribes of one blood, forgive us the bigotry, animosities, hatred, and selfishness that separate us from one another. Because You have redeemed all mankind with the sacrifice of Your only Son, our Lord, make us all one in Him that we may be joined together in His body, the church. Because You have given Your Spirit for bringing all together in the one true faith, knit us together in the fellowship of Christ, in whose name we pray it. Amen.

2

HEAVENLY FATHER, because You will that all men dwell in unity and because You command that we love our neighbors as ourselves, we pray You to forgive the many times we have been separated from our neighbors by bigotry, prejudice, indifference, and apathy. Fill our hearts with Your Spirit that we may be reconciled to our neighbors even as You have reconciled the world to Yourself. Enable us to use our talents and energies to serve the unity or mankind, but above all to help all men to discover their oneness in Christ, our Lord, in whose name we pray it. Amen.

Kingdom Workers

1

HEAVENLY FATHER, help us to realize that it is an honor to serve You. As Your servants we confess our shortcomings and inabilities. We humbly pray You to fill us with a larger measure of Your Spirit. In all our endeavors help us to seek only the honor of Your holy name and the welfare of those who need the sharing of our love. Let no task be considered too small for our devotion. Grant that our courage may not falter when we face those larger opportunities that can be accomplished only through fervent prayer. Remind us that with You nothing is impossible and that without You nothing is worthwhile. Let our good deeds be symbols of gratitude for what You have done for us. Grant that when our work is finished we may all stand in Your presence to enjoy You in Your glory. In the name of our blessed Savior we ask it. Amen.

Ladies Aid or Guild

1

HEAVENLY FATHER, we thank You for having made us Your children by bringing us to faith in Jesus Christ, our Savior. Help us to cherish the privilege of serving You as Your children. Stimulate us to manifest our gratitude to You and our willingness to live for You. In our homes help us do our duty toward our loved ones, and bless all that we do for the strengthening of their faith. Among friends and neighbors teach us to witness by word and deed that we worship at the foot of the cross on Mount Calvary. Bless the work of our organization. Teach us to think and to speak only such things as are pleasing to You and will serve Your holy church. Make us willing to do the work which may be assigned to us today, and bestow Your blessing on our endeavors. We ask it in the name of our Lord and Savior, Jesus Christ. Amen.

2

MOST LOVING FATHER IN HEAVEN, of whom and through whom and to whom are all things — for Thine is the kingdom and the power and the glory — we, Your humble servants, acknowledge our unworthiness to come before You. Because You have invited us to pray and have promised to hear us for the sake of Your Son, Jesus Christ, we make bold to come before Your throne of grace. Endow us with an ever-increasing measure of Your Holy Spirit. Give us all understanding minds and willing hearts to do Your will. May all that we resolve be pleasing to You. Direct us with Your heavenly counsel in our deliberations. Inspire us to do Your holy will not for vainglory but for Him who rendered the supreme sacrifice for our salvation, even Jesus Christ, our Lord and Savior. Amen.

3

O BLESSED LORD JESUS CHRIST, who has promised that if we seek first the kingdom of God and His righteousness, all things needful shall be added to us, grant that our hearts may be enlightened through Your Holy Spirit. Show us the proper pathway of life that leads to the fullness of joy in Your presence forevermore. Teach us to set our affections on those things that are above and that have eternal value. Grant us a spirit of willing service that all our doing and life may please You. Remove far from us all pride and vanity, all envy and covetousness. Cast out of our hearts every evil thought and worldly anxiety. Sanctify us to be dedicated to serve You and Your church. Hear us, O Savior of all mankind, for Your mercy's sake. Amen.

4

LORD JESUS, BLESSED SAVIOR, by Your Holy Spirit make all members of our society to be both Marys and Marthas at the same time. Make us eager to hear Your Word, that we may know what is Your will. Make us zealous to serve You by ministering to the spiritual and physical wants of those who need help. Give us the comforting and sustaining power of Your holy Word. By Your Gospel fill our hearts with the certain faith that our heavenly Father, who delivered You up for us all, will surely with You also freely give us all things we need for life in a troubled and distressed world. May the Holy Spirit guide us by Your Word in ministering to the wants of those in need. Keep us aware of Your glorious promise, that whatever we do to the least of these Your brethren, we do it to You. Hear us, O Lord, and let us feel Your presence in our meeting today. Amen.

5

ALMIGHTY GOD, HEAVENLY FATHER, we begin this meeting in the name of Your dear Son, our Lord and Savior Jesus Christ, through whom alone we can come to You for pardon and peace in the forgiveness of our sins and for strength to do Your will in all things. We confess that by nature we were the children of wrath. We thank You that you have made us Your children by adoption for Jesus' sake. Direct us by Your Holy Spirit to live as Your children. Make us eager to hear You speak to us through Your Word. Show us how to serve

You and our fellowmen, that others may see our good works and so glorify You. May all that we think and say and do in this meeting redound to the glory of Your holy name, for Jesus' sake. Amen.

Married Couples Society

1

O LORD JESUS CHRIST, we thank You for all the blessings of Your saving love and grace which have come to us through our church. We thank You for the privileges of Christian fellowship by which our love and devotion are strengthened and for the opportunities of daily service in our marriage. Grant us a faithful spirit and families of ready obedience to the instruction and direction of Your holy Word. Give us earnest and joyful devotion to the labors of Your church, that in our every action we may serve worthily You, our Lord and King. May Your Spirit guide us in all our deliberations and bless our endeavors, that they may serve the glory of Your name and the welfare of Your church. We ask it for Your love's sake. Amen.

2

O LORD, GOD AND FATHER OF ALL who accept Your salvation through Jesus Christ, we thank You for the love of loved ones, the comfort and shelter of our homes, and the fellowship of our church. All glory and thanks be to You for uniting us in the family of Jesus Christ through faith in His redemption. Bless all the homes of our church through Your Word and Spirit. Remove from our hearts the sins of selfishness, greed, and lovelessness, which exclude You, undermine the home, and destroy happiness. Give us kindness, love, unselfishness, hospitality, and all the graces of the Holy Spirit, that we may dwell and work together in peace and contentment with the members of our families and in the spiritual family of our church. May our meeting result in edifying fellowship with one another and in work accomplished for You, through Jesus Christ, our Lord. Amen.

3

O GOD, we thank You for Your goodness in making us husband and wife, uniting our hearts in creating a common faith, and leading us into the friendship and fellowship of other like-minded couples. We ask Your blessing and benediction on our meeting. Give us strength and security through the awareness of Your presence. Engage us in Your service, and help us grow in Christian love and understanding. As we think, act, and play together, guide our every thought and deed. Through our meeting lead us to a fuller understanding of those things that ennoble and enrich our married lives, and keep us from those things that would mar or blight our marriage. Teach us anew that unless You build our home, we labor in vain in our quest for a healthy and happy home. Use this hour of Christian fellowship, and fortify us in our relationship to You and one another. Yours shall be the kingdom, power and glory. For Jesus' sake. Amen.

4

LORD GOD HEAVENLY FATHER, we join our hearts and minds as we humbly approach Your throne. You have made all things. You have created us and You continue to preserve every good thing for our use. At the very beginning You ordained and sanctified marriage for us.

O Lord Jesus Christ, You honored marriage by Your presence at the wedding feast at Cana, You redeemed our marriage by Your cross.

O Holy Spirit, cleanse our hearts, strengthen and increase our faith. Bring us closer to You and to one another in Christian love. Forgive all we have done wrong. Keep us true and faithful to each other. Bless us, our homes, and our church. Grant us Your presence, and make our society and its work a blessing to us and to others. In Jesus' name we ask it. Amen.

Men's Club

1

O LORD JESUS CHRIST, very God and very man, we thank You for the grace that gives us the power and the faith to face the future with courage and hope in a suffering and dying world. We bless and praise Your holy name for the mercy You have shown us in the forgiveness of our sins. We thank you for the love that has surrounded us from our mother's arms, for the precious gift of faith, and for all the blessings with which You have enriched lives and sustained us through the years. Grant to Christian men everywhere grace to withstand the temptations of the world, the flesh, and the devil. Make us men of prayer, that we might serve You on our knees. Help us to be zealous and faithful soldiers of the Cross ready to fight the good fight of faith. Give us wisdom and understanding, courage and skill to meet the challenge of our opportunities in our own society, congregation, and the church at large. Help us to be faithful to the trust imposed on us. As we are saved by grace through faith, help us, in eternal gratitude, to save others. Bless the labors of our hands. Give power to our testimony through radio, television, or through our own voices in our daily contacts with men. Make us good stewards. Let us reflect Your glory and the peace and joy of the Spirit. We ask it in Your name, for You have bought us with a price and redeemed us to God by Your blood. Amen.

2

"BEHOLD, how good and pleasant it is when brothers dwell in unity!" We thank You, heavenly Father that You have redeemed us by the sacrifice of Your Son and that by Your Holy Spirit You have brought us into fellowship with Your holy church. Grant that as brothers in Christ we love one another with a pure heart fervently. You have assured us that You "give us all things to enjoy" and encouraged us "that every man should eat and drink and enjoy the good of all his labor," therefore let our recreation, discussions, instructions, and all we do redound to Your glory. Above all, make us better stewards to employ well our time, talents, and treasures that we so may do good to all men, especially to those who are of the household of faith. O Lord God, remain always with us and bless us for Your name's sake. Amen.

3

HEAVENLY FATHER we meet in Your name to give attention to ways of serving You. Thankfully we acknowledge Your many blessings on us personally, on our families, and on our congregation. You have called us to the true faith and strengthened our feeble hands times without number. Help us honestly to examine our hearts and minds and rid ourselves of any selfishness and unworthy objectives. Give us grace by Your Holy Spirit to amend our lives and place them now and always in the service of our only Lord and Savior, Jesus Christ. Join us to the whole body of Your saints everywhere in the great work of Your holy church, and grant that we may build well in our own congregation, so that many souls may be won for the heavenly kingdom and eternal life, through Jesus, Your Son, our Lord. Amen.

4

ALMIGHTY GOD OUR HEAVENLY FATHER, as You have called us by Your Spirit to the fellowship of our Lord and Savior Jesus Christ and through Him to fellowship with each other, we thank You for Your gifts of human love and friendship and for the joy that comes from sharing our labors and our recreation with our brethren in Your family. Rule our hearts and govern our behavior that we may build each other up in the faith in speech and conduct revealing that we are Yours. Enable us to know You better and, knowing You, to love You and, loving You, to serve You with glad and willing hearts all the days of this life, until You shall call us into the perfect fellowship of saints and angels in Your heavenly kingdom, through Jesus Christ, our Lord. Amen.

5

LORD JESUS CHRIST, chief Shepherd and Bishop of the church, which You have purchased with Your blood, keep us mindful of the fact that we are a chosen people, made kings and priests to serve God. Enable us to show forth Your praises for having called us out of darkness into Your marvelous light. Look with favor on this men's club as we render service to this congregation and to the church at large. Help us remember that the work which we do is eternal and that the purposes which we serve are Yours. Bestow a special measure of Your grace and wisdom on our officers, and teach us all to yield our will to Your direction. Stimulate us to follow Your example that, losing all thought of self, in humble consecration to Your kingdom's work we may devote our time, talents, and treasures to Your blessed cause and in return enjoy the blessings of Your benediction. Amen.

Mission Committee

1

O MERCIFUL GOD, revealed in the sacrificial love of Your Son, grant us a full measure of Your Holy Spirit. You have called us by the Gospel. Help us give our hearts to You in willing service. Open our eyes to the eternal separation of those who live without Christ. Show us that as we live our life for You, we are instruments of righteousness. Make us and our fellow Christians ready witnesses to Your love in Christ. We pray that the power of the Gospel may reach those grown cold with indifference, those who have resisted the message of Christ, those who have never heard the invitation to believe, and all nations and races and tongues and people, whom You have redeemed with the blood of Christ. Forgive us our selfishness, our lack of interest in soul-winning, and our preoccupation with material projects in the church. Give us a passion for winning souls, for the sake of Jesus Christ, Your Son, our Lord. Amen.

2

O LORD JESUS, as You sent out the Seventy two by two, send us with the same benediction to every corner of our community. We humbly confess our faults. We have given money for missions away from home, but have not given our testimony to our neighbors within reach of our congregation. We have excused our failure to witness by pleading lack of training and ability. We have passed by the unsaved each day without a word of invitation to accept Your love. O Savior, forgive our negligence and our indifference by Your redeeming love. Send us Your Holy Spirit, as on the first Pentecost. Grant that we may be transformed by the fire of Your love. Help us and our fellow Christians to speak Your Word with boldness. Lead us to pray for those who have not been converted to Your way of faith. Grant that we may rely on the power of Your Gospel alone to bring the lost sheep into Your fold. Hear our prayer as You have promised. Amen.

3

O GOD OF OUR SALVATION, WE thank You for
those who led us to Jesus. Let Your Holy Spirit
make every one of us—and those who have
elected us to this Committee—genuine soul-
winners. Grant us a soul-winner's zeal like the
passion for souls that burned within the bosom
of Jesus. Grant us a soul-winner's wisdom that
makes us "wise as serpents and harmless as
doves." Grant us a soul-winner's faith in the
Bible's assurance: "Your labor is not in vain
in the Lord." Grant us a soul-winner's joy like
that of the angels in heaven who rejoice "over
one sinner that repents." Help us ever to proclaim the soul winner's message: "Behold the
Lamb of God, who takes away the sin of the
world." Grant repentance and saving faith to
all who hear that message. We pray in the
name of Jesus. Amen.

4

JESUS, we thank You for saving us from sin.
Make us more thankful. "Restore to us the
joy of Your salvation." Make us restless within

until we are doing our utmost to share the blessing of salvation with others. Help us to lead lost souls to repentance and saving faith in You. Attend the labors of those whom we have sent to go where we cannot go. Fill them and us with a passion for souls. Give them and us wisdom and tact in dealing with those who know You not. Protect them and us from harm. Preserve them and us in good health. Bless their labors and ours. Let many voices be added to the choirs that will sing Your praises forever. To that end grant us Your guidance and grant us success in our present undertakings. Amen.

5

DIVINE REDEEMER, because You gave Your life that all men might be the heirs of everlasting life, we beseech You to enrich this meeting with Your presence. Give the guidance of Your Holy Spirit as we ponder plans to establish Your Cross everywhere to bring Your Gospel to the far reaches of the earth. Make us eager and zealous to dare in faith what seems difficult and beyond our strength. Give us the words and help us be examples to inspire our fellow Christians to bring the sacrifices needed for the work of missions. Move them by Your divine compassion to enlist in harvesting the dearly redeemed so that the borders of Zion may be enlarged to include a conquering host. Bless our humble efforts in grace and may all we plan and do glorify You before men who shall praise our God eternally. Amen.

6

LORD JESUS, we stand at Your cross, humbly grateful for the grace and mercy manifested to us. By Your Holy Spirit inflame us with zeal to bear witness to Your redemption. Help us to plan and toil that we may share Your mercies with others who are enshrouded in the darkness of sin. Enable us by word and deed to bear eloquent and enduring testimony to You. Help us to overcome an unwilling spirit, so that we shall inspire our fellow believers to enlist under Your mandate, "You shall be My witnesses." Enable us to give of time and treasure so that Your kingdom may truly come among us. May we go forth into a sin-cursed and dying world, resolved to know no rest until we have sought to carry Your Gospel into every place where You Yourself would come. These petitions we ask in Your name for the glory of our God. Amen.

7

LORD JESUS, in Your love for the salvation of the world You have taught us to pray: "Thy kingdom come." By Your Holy Spirit teach us to know the meaning of this petition. Help us be more fervently concerned about our own salvation. Grant us greater diligence in the use of the means of grace for the strengthening of our faith and daily improvement in newness of life. Let this holy kingdom, Your blessed reign of grace, come to others also. May it be spread throughout the world. May thousands upon thousands partake of its blessings. To that end grant us wisdom and courage to speak Your Word to others. Make us and all Your people willing to pray, work, and give for Your holy cause. Bless all our missionaries, pastors, and teachers. According to Your promise let Your kingdom come and

Your will be done for in Your holy name we pray. Amen.

8

GRACIOUS GOD AND FATHER the glorious work of saving souls is Yours, and in Your condescending love You have called and commissioned us to be "workers together with You" in this great work, to use us as instruments in bringing to others the message of Your redeeming and saving love in Christ. Help us appreciate the glorious privilege and the tremendous responsibility this high calling places on us. Fill our hearts with fervor and determination to bring the Gospel to all people in all parts of the world who are still without Christ and without hope. Make us willing to labor zealously for this high and holy cause to dedicate ourselves with all that we are and have to the work of Christian missions. Hear us and help us for Jesus' sake. Amen.

9

MERCIFUL SAVIOR, by Your Holy Spirit You have granted us grace, through faith in You and Your Word to become members of Your kingdom in which we have the assurance of the forgiveness of our sins and our final salvation in heaven. In this experience of Your undeserved favor may we be mindful of the uncounted millions who do not yet enjoy these blessings. Mercifully forgive us our indifference and negligence for not having done all that we could have done to bring them Your saving Gospel. As You came "not to be served but to serve and to give Your life as a ransom for many," grant us the love and faith to deny ourselves in faithful service for the extension of Your kingdom. Bestow on us the will to do all we can by word and deed to carry out Your command to "preach the Gospel to every creature." We ask this for Your name's sake. Amen.

Mothers Club

1

"CHARM IS DECEITFUL, and beauty is vain, but a woman who fears the Lord is to be praised." Eternal and almighty God, the Source of life and in whom alone true fulfillment of life can be found, with humble hearts and reverent minds we come to You for Your blessing. We thank You for the gracious gift of life which You have given us, for a mother's arm to hold us, a mother's love to enfold us, and a mother's care and tenderness to provide for us. Especially we thank You for the greatest gift of all, Your only begotten Son, born of a woman, through whom we have become Your children. By sending Him in the flesh, You hallowed womanhood and childhood. We praise You for all godly mothers who have shared with their children their holy faith. Fill them with an ever deeper sense of responsibility for the children You have given them. Help them train their children in the ways of Him who alone is the Truth, the Life, and the Way. Help them be wise counselors and true companions. Make them patient and untiring in all their labors with You to make Christlike men and women for tomorrow's world. Grant them the compensation of a love returned. Fill them with the satisfaction of knowing that they have lifted up those entrusted to them into harmony with Your eternal plans and purposes. We make our prayer in the name of Jesus, our Lord, who from the cross remembered His mother and by His sacrifice redeemed all motherhood. Amen.

2

DEAR FATHER IN HEAVEN, we ask Your guidance for our gathering. You alone have called us to the high and holy vocation of motherhood, and we come to You humbly conscious of our unworthiness, asking that You bless us. Breathe into our hearts the spirit of Your grace, and enable us faithfully to fulfill our duty to You and to those whom You have placed in our care. Through Your Word endow us with wisdom and restrain us from impatience. Give us understanding hearts to share the griefs and anxieties of others, sympathy and prudence to guide and counsel in times of perplexity. Let us remember that as we seek Your kingdom and righteousness first, all else will be added unto us. Trusting in Your fatherly goodness we beseech Your blessing on us, that the solving of our problems redound to Your glory and the welfare of those who need our love. We ask this in Jesus' name. Amen.

3

DEAR HEAVENLY FATHER, as we consider the problems and needs of those who are near and dear to us, we come to You seeking help and guidance. Keep us and our loved ones by Your Holy Spirit faithful to You and Your church. Grant us at all times wisdom and understanding to train our children in Your faith and fear. Give us the necessities to provide for our daily wants, and grant us humility to rely on Your promises in the assurance that You know what is best. Guide us by Your Word to live always as Your children, bought with the precious blood of Your Son Jesus Christ. Help us grow in Your Word that we may be true examples of Christlikeness in our homes, to our children, and to all people. Relieve the burdens and grief of mothers everywhere through Jesus Christ, our Lord, who showed His love for His mother from the cross and by the cross redeemed all motherhood. In His name we pray. Amen.

4

LORD JESUS, Shepherd of the lambs of Your flock, we are all too often weak in our resolve to serve as Christian mothers. Forgive us our past sins. Strengthen us by Your Spirit through the holy Gospel and the sacraments. Grant us wisdom to recognize our responsibilities as parents, courage to accept our limitations and shortcomings, charity and understanding as we entrust our children to sincere, well-trained Christian teachers, and the insight to realize that our children reflect their homes. As mothers once brought their children to You, so we bring our children to Your loving arms for forgiveness and blessing. Grant success to the earnest efforts of church, school, and home in bringing up our children in Your nurture and admonition. Bless the endeavors and decisions of our mothers' club so that Your kingdom may prosper and Your holy name be glorified among us. We pray in deepest humility, merciful Redeemer, because You have purchased us and our children with Your holy, precious blood to make us Your own in time and in eternity. Amen.

Outdoor Meeting

LORD GOD ALMIGHTY, Maker of all that lives
and moves and has being, Creator of this uni-
verse, of all that is seen and unseen, we give
our thanks for Your bounty and goodness. We
thank You for the beauties of nature, the
snow-capped mountain peaks and the hush of
a quiet wayside pond, the flowers and the
forests, and for every good gift. We confess our
unworthiness and inadequacy. We cannot fully
appreciate or understand Your goodness and
greatness. May we ever remember the glory
of Your creation and with humble wonder
contemplate Your world. We ask You to be
with us as we meet in the outdoors. May our
fellowship be blessed by the presence of the
Holy Spirit. May our Savior Jesus Christ, who
frequently sought the quiet solace of nature,
be our Companion. May all we say and do be
hallowed by the faith that everything comes
from Your hands and is Your sole creation.

Bless our meeting, our deliberations, and our recreation in the same bountiful way You have blessed the world. We praise and thank You, the eternal God, in the name of Your Son Jesus Christ, our Redeemer. Amen.

Parent-Teacher Association

1

DEAR HEAVENLY FATHER, who through Your Son has commanded us to teach all nations, we seek Your light and guidance in the performance of our duties in providing for the proper instruction of the children who have been placed under our care and direction. Give us wisdom and insight that we may do nothing amiss. Give us willingness and zeal to establish and extend Your work. Give us love to bind us together in our common service. Bless all who teach and all who learn, that Your name may be glorified. Hear us for Jesus' sake. Amen.

2

LORD, we recognize that You have bountifully blessed our Christian homes and (school and) Sunday School. We thank You for the privilege of teaching the rising generation of children, that they may know You and set their hope in You. Keep us from becoming careless about our task, and help us to supply our children's bodily and spiritual needs according to Your good pleasure. Show us how best to instruct them in divine wisdom, how to admonish them when they sin, and how to comfort them when sin or other sorrow burdens their hearts. Strengthen us in our common task. Help us to set a good example at all times, so that our actions may not nullify our instruction and admonition. Grant grace to the children under our care that they may grow up as firm believers in You and that they may cheerfully serve You. Make them obedient to parents and teachers and useful to their homes, their church, and their nation. May they be a joy to You and to Christians everywhere. Let none of our children go astray, and bring them with us into Your glorious presence, in Jesus' name. Amen.

3

DEAR FATHER IN HEAVEN, we thank You for the blessing of children and for the privilege of being Christian parents and teachers. Help us to recognize both our responsibility and our opportunity to serve You and our children. Give us wisdom in dealing with the problems of child training, strength to persevere when difficulties arise, patience when disappointments or sorrows come, and love in dealing with our children and with each other. Bless our homes and our school (Sunday school) in Your work, and help us to labor peacefully together to the glory of Your name and to the eternal welfare of ourselves and our children. Enlighten our hearts that we may always seek right and oppose wrong, and move also the hearts of the children under our care that they may believe in You and willingly submit to Your will. When we or our children sin, graciously forgive, and at Your own time bring us to our eternal home above, for Jesus' sake. Amen.

4

DEAR GOD, impress on us the earnestness of Your command regarding our children: "Bring them up in the nurture and admonition of the Lord." Give us wise and understanding hearts that we may always recognize our great responsibility to lead these precious souls to Jesus and to do all to keep them in the Savior's fold. Make our homes Your workshops. We thank You for the support that our congregation provides to assist parents in their vital task of Christian youth training, and we humbly implore You to bless the work and the workers of these agencies (the Christian day school, Sunday school . . .) with Your grace and favor. Use us to stand by them with our fervent prayers, our sincere interest, and our wholehearted cooperation. Faithful Father, keep Your protecting hand over our homes and schools. Holy Jesus, embrace us with Your love and forgiveness. Sacred Spirit, turn our eyes and hearts ever more steadfastly to the Cross, and bless us with Your power and peace. Amen.

5

HEAVENLY FATHER, as parents and teachers we are assembled in Your name. You have entrusted to our care and special concern the training and Christian education of children. We tremble at the responsibility that is ours when we think of the value You have placed on the soul of one of these little ones. You have redeemed them through Jesus Christ, Your Son, our Savior. In Baptism their sins are washed away; and they are delivered from sin, death, and the power of the devil. We humbly acknowledge our own imperfections and shortcomings to serve as Your representatives to the children for whom we are responsible. Relying on Your promise, we come to You for help and guidance. Make us worthy examples and patterns for the children to follow. Be present, O Holy Spirit, in our meeting. Let all that we think or say or resolve to do be for the welfare of Your dear children and to the glory of Your most holy name, through Jesus Christ. Amen.

6

DEAR FATHER IN HEAVEN, You have entrusted precious children to our care. We thank You for the joy they have brought to us, their parents and teachers. We ask You to be with us in caring for them and training them. Bless us with the means to provide for their physical needs. In this day that has multiplied the dangers and temptations surrounding the youth, especially guide us and bless us in providing for their mental and spiritual training. Grant, heavenly Father, that we avoid educational programs that train only for this life. Help us provide for them an education that will cause them to be consecrated Christians, useful citizens in this world, and worthy subjects of Your heavenly kingdom through Jesus Christ, their Savior. May the grace of our Lord Jesus Christ and the love of God and the communion of the Holy Spirit be with us always. Amen.

Parish or High School

Precious Jesus, Fountain of all knowledge, be with us as we concern ourselves with the continued welfare of this parish (high) school. We gratefully acknowledge its establishment as one of Your blessings and implore You to preserve it as Your instrument in leading our precious youth to You, their Savior. Give our teaching staff a special measure of Your Spirit, that they may approach the problems of youth with sympathy and understanding. Enable them to guide eager and inquiring minds beyond the things that are seen and temporal to the things that are unseen and eternal. May the products of this school be a generation of Your trusting followers, Your consecrated workers, and Your prayerful, loyal citizens. Surrounded by special dangers and weaknesses, may our youth find in You "the victory that overcomes the world." Fill our hearts with faith and courage to extend our school's blessings to others. Prosper us in our endeavors to enlarge its influence. Teach us to remember that Your commission: "Teach them!" is also filled with the promise: "I am with you always!" Amen.

Planning Committee

1

LORD JESUS, as Head and Governor of the church, who would have all things done decently and in order, we humbly pray You to be with us and guide us in our planning. Give us good insight and understanding of the tasks and problems confronting our church today, so that together we may strive to solve these problems in Your fear and to Your glory. Widen our horizon, and give us good perspective so that we may recognize the golden opportunities for soul-saving that lie ahead and then together plan to make the most of them. And when You have given us the vision and warmed our hearts anew, grant us the grace to relay to others, especially to the groups in which we are the chosen leaders, the things that we have heard and seen. Thus may we as a congregation go forward with one heart and mind, that Your kingdom may come and Your will be done among us. We ask this humbly for Your name's sake. Amen.

2

HEAVENLY FATHER, who in Your mercy made us members of one Christian family and entrusted to us the task of planning the work of our church, we ask Your grace and guidance in our meeting. As You "called us in one hope of our calling," give us unity of heart and mind as we consider the tasks and opportunities of our church at home and abroad. Help us realize that in unity there is strength and that as we think and act together Your church will be able to move forward like a mighty army. Since without vision a people perishes, give us good perspective and vision, that we may anticipate the course of our church in these coming months and plan and prepare for those things that lie ahead. When we have made our plans, open our lips that we may share our enthusiasm and our convictions with those who have been entrusted to our leadership. As

You are ever present with those who gather in Your name, be with us and let Your benediction rest on all that we do or say. For Your name's sake. Amen.

Scout Camp Service

WE THANK YOU, dear heavenly Father, for the privilege of worshiping You this Lord's Day among the wonders of nature. As we behold the glories of Your handiwork all about us, draw us into a more intimate communion with You. May Your Word this day fall on attentive ears and take root in believing hearts. Inspire us to lift our voices in joyful hymns of praise to You. Make us diligent and fervent in our prayers at Your throne of grace. Help us to go forth from this service strengthened and inspired for a life consecrated to You and our fellowman. Teach us in the days of youth to give You the firstfruits of our lives. And enable us day by day to grow up into the full stature of Christian manhood and womanhood until one day, made acceptable alone by the merits of Christ, we shall be received to heavenly glory. In Jesus' name we ask this. Amen.

Scout Troop Meeting

LORD JESUS, graciously look with favor on our Scout activities. Help us faithfully to use our individual talents and skills to Your glory, the help of our fellowman, and the improvement of our community. Preserve us from the sins of youth. Shield us in the hour of temptation. Keep us pure in heart, upright in life, and diligent in all our tasks. As You have left us an example of obedience to Your parents in the days of Your youth, grant us grace at all times to respect authority and to be subject to elders and superiors. Enable us to cultivate every Christian virtue and in all things to grow up in You. Looking to You, the Author and Finisher of our faith, may we go from strength to strength, till at last, having finished our course and kept the faith, we may receive from You the crown of life that fades not away. For Your blessed name's sake we ask this. Amen.

Stewardship Committee

1

O LORD, HEAVENLY FATHER, because You will
require much from those to whom You have
given much, grant that we who know the fullness of Your mercy by grace may give a good
account of the love You have showered on us
by rendering full service to others, that in
serving others we may know the joy of serving
You through Jesus Christ, Your Son, our
Lord. Amen.

2

GRACIOUS FATHER, because You have given to
our congregation the blessing of many gifts,
many talents, and much treasure, help us to
inspire one another and the whole congregation to use all that we have in Your service.

100

Help us to pool the resources of our health and wealth, our affluence and influence for the good of the church and the welfare of many according to Your will and for the sake of Jesus, our Lord. Amen.

3

HEAVENLY FATHER, because You work without tiring for us in love, because You sent our Lord Jesus Christ to work out our salvation for us, and because You gave Your Holy Spirit to make us Your co-workers, enable us to labor diligently as Your fellow workers. Help us to lead our congregation to be good stewards of what You have entrusted to us, that we may multiply the love You have given us with the goods You have loaned us to serve the welfare of many in the name of Christ, our Lord. Amen.

Student Group

1

GRACIOUS GOD, we confess that we sometimes use prayer as a pious, almost meaningless method to begin a meeting or convocation. Make this prayer and this meeting different. With the psalmist of old we implore, "Create in me a clean heart, O God, and renew a right spirit within me." We rededicate to You our personalities, our gifts and talents, our loves and friendships, our money and material possessions. With the faith that we are completely Yours no matter who we are or what we have done, we come into Your holy presence. We are grateful that You have knit us together in Christian friendship and have kindled in us an interest in one another's welfare. We are thankful that we may be together again for worship, study, and fellowship. Cause us to appreciate more and more how much we need each other as fellow Christians. As we participate in Your program, may each of us be drawn closer to You, and through You closer to one another. May holiness of living be reflected in our daily living on the campus, in our dormitories and residences, and in our classrooms. We thank You deeply for the privilege of higher education, for professors dedicated to their work and to us, for parents who have given of themselves to us, for friends and sweethearts without whom life is lonely and empty, and most of all for Your Son, without whom life would be impossible.

In the name of the Father who created us, the Son who redeemed us from our sinfulness and death, and the Holy Spirit who brought us to faith and keeps us in it! Amen.

2

LORD GOD, because You know how we struggle with problems of identity, vocation, support, and meaning, help us by Your Holy Spirit to find ourselves in Christ, our Lord, to recognize when You call us to service through Your neighbor, to rely completely on Your providence, and to give meaning to all things through the redeeming love of our Savior. In His name we pray. Amen.

Sunday School Conference

1

ALMIGHTY AND MOST GRACIOUS GOD, the Father of our Lord Jesus Christ, as You have commanded us to pray that You send laborers into Your harvest, we thank and praise You that You have chosen us to be teachers of Your Word and workers in the Sunday schools of the church. Put Your saving Gospel into our hearts and on our lips. Enable us to carry out Your will and to teach Your holy Word with all diligence. Empower young and old, being instructed, nurtured, comforted, and strengthened by Your Word, to grow in grace and knowledge and to do those things that are well-pleasing to You. Direct us this day in all our doing with Your most gracious Spirit, and further us with Your continual help, that in all our work begun, continued, and ended in You we may glorify Your holy name and may bring many to the saving knowledge of life in Christ Jesus, our Lord. In His name we pray. Amen.

2

HEAVENLY FATHER, we come to You in the name of Jesus, humbly asking You to bless us in behalf of the Sunday schools of our church. You have committed to us Your precious Word of reconciliation and the teaching of Your statutes. Grant that we who lead and teach others may ever be taught and led by You. Forgive us all our failings of the past, and fill us with a full measure of Your Spirit. May all whom we are privileged to teach be inspired by Your Spirit and instructed by Your heavenly wisdom. Bless our conference today to the end that we with our weak efforts at Sunday school work may become more useful to You. For Your gracious love in Christ Jesus, our blessed Savior, we adore You, O God. For the riches in Christ that have come to us, we praise and thank You, O Lord. May all that we think and say and do this day glorify You. Amen.

Sunday School Session

1

LORD JESUS, as we meet this morning in Sunday school, we remember Your word, "Feed My sheep" and "Feed My lambs." We pray You, give to all of us the blessing of Your Holy Spirit that we may walk in the green pastures of Your holy Word. Give us the willingness to listen to You and to live according to Your teachings. Open Your hand in blessing on us all, that our Sunday school may always be a beautiful garden of grace where the fragrance of Your love and the beauty of Your righteousness may cause us to walk in daily repentance and faith. Give to our teachers such understanding and knowledge that Your Word may be taught simply and effectively. Give to us, both pupils and learners, such attention and interest that we may be conscious of Your presence always and lay hold on the things needful for our eternal salvation. In Your name we pray it. Amen.

2

HEAVENLY FATHER, we thank You for the Holy Bible, in which You have spoken so plainly to us. We are thankful for our teachers and our leaders, who desire to serve You and us in the teaching of Your truth. We pray as we gather for our Sunday school this morning, as boys and girls, as men and women, as teachers and pupils, that we may glorify You in our worship and in our lesson period. We ask You for Jesus' sake to forgive us our sins. Bless our lesson study that we may know and do Your will. Be with those who cannot be with us because of illness. Bless all our Sunday schools in our churches here at home and those in far-off lands. We earnestly pray You for these blessings in the name of Jesus Christ, Your Son, our Lord. Amen.

3

How PRECIOUS is our privilege, O merciful God, to be assembled in Your name and upon Your gracious invitation! We have come here to receive knowledge of Your holy Word and will, to be strengthened in the saving faith, and by Your love to be stirred up for a more consecrated life and devoted service to You. Remove from us all spiritual blindness and indifference, and grant us understanding and appreciation of those blessings which have lasting value. By the power of Your Gospel promises move us joyfully to accept Your truth and to do those things that will please You and further Your cause. Inspire us to witness boldly and patiently of Your truth and grace, so that our testimony in Word and life may direct precious souls to You for guidance, strength, and hope. We ask it in Jesus' name. Amen.

4

LORD JESUS, OUR SAVIOR AND FRIEND, we have come to meet with You according to Your promise, "Where two or three are gathered together in My name, there am I in the midst of them," and to receive the lasting blessings of Your precious Word. Graciously accept our praise and thanksgiving, which we with united hearts and lips bring before You for all Your mercies and love, which You have granted daily to us, Your servants. Open our hearts to Your life-giving Word that it may work with power to direct and sanctify our minds and lives and fill them with pure wisdom and saving faith. Unite our hearts to fear Your name and to cherish Your truth. Teach us to know the road we should walk, and lead us in right paths and in the way everlasting. Direct us in our daily life to share joyfully with everyone these good gifts, which by grace You grant to us, Your servants. We ask it in Your blessed name. Amen.

5

LORD JESUS, OUR BLESSED REDEEMER, we thank and praise You for having saved us by the shedding of Your precious blood on the cross. Because You have revealed Your love in Your Word and have willed that we should know the Gospel and commanded that we should search the Scriptures, help us to learn of You in our study. Grant us Your gracious presence as we study Your Word in our Sunday school lesson today. Lead and move us by Your Holy Spirit that we may ever cling to You as our only Savior, learn to love You more, and serve You with a willing heart. We pray in Your name. Amen.

6

OUR HEAVENLY FATHER, we are gathered here in Your name to study and learn Your precious Word. By nature we are blind and ignorant in spiritual matters. We need You and Your Holy Spirit to lead and guide us into all truth. We therefore humbly pray You for the gift of Your Spirit, that He may enlighten our minds to accept and believe Your Word and fill our hearts with new love and devotion to serve You with gladness and untiring zeal. Hear us, we pray You, for the sake of Your love, which You have revealed to us in Christ Jesus, our Lord and Savior. Amen.

7

HEAVENLY FATHER, as in loving-kindness You provide daily bread for people on earth, we thank You that You have graciously supplied all our needs during the past week. You have sustained us in both body and mind. You have defended us from all dangers. You have given us shelter and daily bread. Above all, You have kept us mindful of the boundless love that caused You to send Your Son, Jesus Christ, to take our place and suffer the punishment of death that we had earned by our sins. We, who believe in Him as our Savior and know that we shall never perish but have everlasting life, thank You for such sin-forgiving grace. As we are assembled in our Sunday school, give us attentive ears and eager spirits to study Your holy Word faithfully so that we may love You more and serve You better. We ask this in the name of our holy Savior, Jesus Christ. Amen.

8

LORD GOD, HEAVENLY FATHER, we are gathered together in Your name to learn the precious

Word of life. In that Word by Your Holy Spirit continue to teach us that we do not deserve Your grace and favor. Cleanse us daily from our sins through the precious blood of Jesus, who gave His life that we might never die. Draw us close to You in love and devotion. Lead us in the way that leads to everlasting life. Keep us faithful to Your Word, which is a lamp unto our feet. As You have called us to salvation through the saving Gospel, so teach us to realize that this Gospel is also intended to be a light to all people. Fill us with a desire and a determination to tell our friends and neighbors of the salvation that comes through Your Word, that Your kingdom may come and Your will be done. We ask this in the name of Jesus. Amen.

Sunday School
Teachers Meeting

1

LORD JESUS CHRIST, You have given to Your
disciples everywhere and in all ages the command to bring the little children to You. You
gave the apostle Peter and to us the commission to feed Your lambs. You have made us
workers in Your vineyard to bring Your saving
Gospel to the youth of the church and of our
community. May we, as Your humble learners
and followers, teach Your holy Word in season
and out of season by all our words and all our
doings. Bless our study of the Holy Bible now,
that we, rightly dividing the Word of truth,
may more and more become workers of whom
You will never be ashamed. Give us the
precious, enlightening gift of Your Holy Spirit,

and establish the work of our hands in our Sunday school; yea, the work of our hands, establish it. Amen.

2

HEAVENLY FATHER, we thank and praise You for having given us Your holy Word in which You have revealed Your love to us sinners in giving Your only-begotten Son to be for us a Savior from sin and hell. We confess that we are insufficient of ourselves to teach diligently to our children. We need You and Your Spirit. Grant us an ever richer measure of Your Holy Spirit, that in the study of Your Word He may enlighten our minds and strengthen our faith so that we may ever steadfastly trust in Your mercy and serve You with grateful hearts all our days. To that end bless us now as we search and learn Your holy Word, in Jesus' name. Amen.

3

LORD JESUS, our adorable and only Savior, we praise and glorify Your holy name for having redeemed us poor, lost, and condemned sinners from all sins, from death, and from the power of the devil. You have loved us and given Yourself for us. We thank You for the wonders of Your great love. What may we do to repay Your love? We are saved to serve. Here and now we reconsecrate ourselves to You and Your holy service. Grant us a rich measure of Your Holy Spirit, that He may lead and guide us into all truth. As we now study Your precious Gospel, enlighten our minds to understand Your Word and truly to believe it. Fill our hearts with new zeal and devotion to love You and serve You with joy, for Your name's sake. Amen.

4

LORD JESUS, give us Your heart to love children, Your mind to understand them, Your will to serve them. In the surrender of our self to You may we find joy in doing our Father's will. Forgive us when we grow weary of our work, neglect it, or become impatient with those we teach. Enrich us with grace to perform with cheer, sympathy, devotion, and humility the task You have committed to our trust. Help us to make You known. May we be persuasive examples of Your compassion for sinners and convincing witnesses to Your gracious salvation. Do not allow our weaknesses to stand in the way of Your Word. Savior and King, may we possess You in our lives, and having You, may we share You with those for whom You have given Yourself. Amen.

Women's Missionary Guild or League

1

HEAVENLY FATHER, we praise You for Your many mercies, which are new every morning. Humbly we confess our sins, our inadequacies, our lack of love. Forgive us, O Lord, and give us the power of Your Spirit to rise above our selfishness to the level of the high calling that is ours in Christ Jesus. Grant us an ever-increasing measure of Your Spirit. Endow us with the Christian knowledge of Priscilla, the faithfulness of Mary Magdalene, the prayerfulness of Hannah, the willingness of Ruth, and the zealousness of the Samaritan woman who went to tell others about Jesus. Be with us in this meeting with Your divine presence. Increase our faith. Inspire us by Your Word to hear Your Macedonian call everywhere. Consecrate our hands, our voices, our lips, and our gifts of love in the service of saving souls for You. In Jesus' name we pray. Amen.

2

DEAR HEAVENLY FATHER, because You have given Your beloved Son to die for a lost world, we thank You for bringing us to believe in Him as our Savior and to love and serve Him as our Lord. We bless You for giving us this opportunity of meeting together as a women's missionary league. Help us to grow in the knowledge of our far-flung missions. Grant us new fervor and zeal to witness for You. Give us thankful hearts and willing hands to contribute gladly and liberally. Bless our study of Your Word and our discussion of missionary topics. Bestow Your benediction on all the projects of our league, our congregation, and our church. With divine protection watch over our workers and their families who in our stead have gone to the ends of the earth. Give success to Your Word, for the extension of Your kingdom, the salvation of many souls, and the glory of Your name, through Jesus Christ, our Lord. Amen.

3

Dear Lord and Savior Jesus Christ, who has charged us to publish salvation everywhere, we ask Your guidance and blessing for our missionary league meeting. We thank You for showing so often in the Scriptures that our souls are precious and our services are acceptable to You. Bless our society and our nationwide association of witnessing believers, with all our officers and members, and make us a power working for You. Accept and multiply our offerings and mite boxes for the erection of many churches where Your Cross will be proclaimed. Give us the spirit of consecration and stewardship that knows no limit and holds nothing back from You, because You give us all. Help us to go forth from this meeting with a fuller understanding of our task, a growing love toward the lost, and an increased training for Your service, for the sake of Your love to us, our life's greatest incentive. Amen.

4

Lord Jesus, we meet to do the work You have assigned us. It is Your work. May all that we do please You. Make us remember Your great humility, that we seek not our own honor and pleasure but that which pleases and honors You. Teach us to learn. Move us to love. Inspire us to work so that those who know You not may join us at the foot of Your cross. Bless our work to Your pleasure, and direct our efforts to Your glory. Help us to make the angels sing as souls are won through Your salvation. Your promises to us are sure. Send Your Holy Spirit to be with us in our meeting, that all we think, do, and say may truly serve to enlarge Your work. Direct all our desires to that end. We ask it of our Father, in Your name. Amen.

5

LORD OF ALL MANKIND, in Jesus You have given us a perfect Savior and through Him made us partakers of heaven. You have honored us by appointing us to tell others of the salvation Christ has won for all men. Make us alert to the needs of those who do not know Him and His salvation. Direct our understanding to help them and to serve You. Strengthen our hands that our labors for Your kingdom be worthy of Your purposes. Touch our hearts to love You and lost sinners, whom You love. To this end, O Lord, bless our deliberations this day. Be present with us. Direct us by Your wisdom. Correct our errors. Guide us in mercy. Inspire us by Your love. Let all we do be for the welfare of men's souls and to Your glory. We ask it in the name of Jesus, our Savior. Amen.

6

O DEAR LORD JESUS, Savior of all mankind, You have commanded us to be witnesses for You before men so that they might come to the saving faith. Since we are met for the purpose of becoming more proficient in testifying of You, we pray You to give us an abundant measure of Your Holy Spirit, that our study and our discussion in this meeting may prove beneficial to us and through us to others. Grant that we love You more dearly, and make us more grateful to You for Your great sacrifice on the cross, so that we may be more eager to confess Your name before men and that out of a greater fullness of our hearts we speak to them of You as their only Savior from sin and the only Way to the Father and to heaven. Hear our petitions for the sake of Your own merits. Amen.

7

O Holy Spirit, we thank You that in Your mercy and grace You have brought us to the saving faith in Christ Jesus as our all-sufficient Savior from sin. Strengthen us in this faith, and give us an increase of knowledge and of understanding of the great truths revealed in the Holy Scriptures. Grant us the further grace to make progress in the sanctification of life, avoiding that which is displeasing to You and becoming richer in the doing of good works. So direct us that by our conduct and by our confession, by our life and by our lips, we show forth in growing measure the praises of our eternally blessed Redeemer. To this end grace our meeting with Your presence and bountifully bless our deliberations. We ask this in the name of Jesus, our only Savior. Amen.

Young Adults

1

O GOD, the Giver of all light, help us to walk as children of light. Bless our organization in its efforts to be a beacon of Your light in the community and the church. May we reflect the love, the grace, and the mercy You have given us in Christ Jesus, that our activities may further the cause of His Gospel and serve the welfare of His church for the benefit of many. In His name we pray. Amen.

2

LORD GOD, we commend ourselves to You and to Your will. Energize us by Your Spirit that we may pursue Your purpose in all things we do together. Give us ingenuity and creativity in doing new things for You and each other. Make us bold for the sake of Your church and willing to serve one another. Help us deepen our relationships that together we may give honor to Your holy name through Jesus Christ, our Lord. Amen.

Youth Group

1

ALMIGHTY GOD, LORD OF ALL MANKIND, behold us, Your children, as we gather to plan and work for that which pleases You. We are deeply conscious of our shortcomings. Many times we have not done the things You would have us do to Your glory and the welfare of all men. We know we are apt to forget You as we go about our tasks. For this forgetfulness of You and Your tasks grant us Your gracious forgiveness. Clothe us with the whole armor of defense against sin and temptation. Give us Your truth as our belt, Your righteousness as our breastplate, and the Gospel of peace as our footgear. Put on us the helmet of salvation, and let us firmly hold the sword of Your Spirit, the Word of God. Give us a strong faith as our shield. As we go about our tasks in our fellowship, enable us to overcome our weakness and to press forward in the army of Your marching saints on earth. As we assemble in Your name, make us to know more certainly that everything can be done only with Your benediction poured out upon us. We ask this because Jesus, our Savior, has taught us to come to Your heavenly throne in His name and for His sake. Amen.

2

DEAR HEAVENLY FATHER, in this hour of work and fellowship we ask that Your presence be a glorious reality for us. We confess that too many times we have neglected the tasks You have given us. Where we should have been enthusiastic, we were indifferent. Where we should have been eager, we were lazy. For these shortcomings we ask Your forgiveness for the sake of Your Son, Jesus Christ, the Shepherd of youth, who offered Himself for us on Calvary. Now we ask in all confidence that Your blessings rest on us, on our decisions, on our tasks, and on our fellowship. Give us holy zeal and inspired enthusiasm for the cause of Your holy church. May we never forget that we are in this world to do Your will, and may we ever remember that without Your help and love we are nothing. This we ask for in the name of Jesus, our Savior, who loves us and died for us. Amen.

3

DEAR FATHER IN HEAVEN, hear this prayer of our young hearts. We are thankful to grow up in this age of progress. We recognize that every blessing of home, industry, school, and community is directly from Your loving hands. But, O Lord, this age of speed and change and new things has its dangers. We often forget You and Your purpose in our lives. We attach ourselves to the pleasures and ideals of the world too much. Forgive us. We ask You, therefore, to help us as we gather in Your name. Enable us to pull our thoughts to Your way of thinking and our life to Your way of living. Above all, we pray that You would fill our hearts, minds, and bodies with the love, hope, and life that come only from knowing Jesus Christ as Savior. Teach us to rely on Him and His promises of wisdom and strength, so that our worship, work, and relaxation may be godly and useful. We humbly speak this prayer in His most holy name. Amen.

4

(Based on the Aims of a Youth Organization. It may be read responsively.)

To assist in keeping our young people in the fellowship of Your church: **We need Your help, O Lord.**

To promote growth among all youth in understanding and use of Your Word: **We need Your help, O Lord.**

To assist one another in preparation for a life of service to You and mankind: **We need Your help, O Lord.**

To develop an active love for the announcement of forgiveness through Christ to all near at hand and afar off: **We need Your help, O Lord.**

To foster godliness and true enjoyment in our social life and recreation: **We need Your help, O Lord.**

To encourage gifts and acts of service to all less fortunate than ourselves: **We need Your help, O Lord.**

To build close ties and deep loyalties to our Christian homes: **We need Your help, O Lord.**

To guide one another through organized youth activities in our congregation: **We need Your help, O Lord.**

To unite all youth who love You, the only true God, and Jesus Christ, whom You have sent: **We need Your help, O Lord.**

5

O LIVING GOD, as You have guided the youth of every age, we ask Your presence and power at our meeting. Help us to understand ourselves, our pride and self-consciousness, our enthusiasm and laziness. Teach us to see more clearly the love, forgiveness, and peace that we have through Jesus Christ, our Savior. In the fast-moving days of our youth, enable us to think of You, of Your church, and of Your will. May our life with our parents, our teachers, our

friends, our fellow workers display the changed
heart that we have by the power of Your Spirit.
As we call on Your name, be pleased to fill us
with interest for our daily assignments, chores,
and duties. Inspire us with love for one another
and all men. Deepen our faith in Your promises, through Jesus Christ. Amen.

6

WE in these days of our youth are Yours, O
Father. Bless what we do in Your name. Help
us grow daily in the practice of prayer and in
the understanding of Your Word. Make Your
love for us in Christ be personal and mean-
ingful. Show us the importance of our Christian life in this confused world. Lead us to
witness to our oneness with You by word and
deed. Bring us closer to all those who love
Christ, especially the members of our own congregation. Make us ready to forgive, willing
to help, and eager to work together for Your
kingdom. Remind us of our fellowship with
Jesus as we play and seek amusements, that
all of our life may be good and godly. Add Your
blessing to our plans and projects. May Your

holy angels remain at hand in all our ways. In the name of Your Son, our Savior and Lord. Amen.

7

ALMIGHTY GOD, as You have given us life by Your creating hand, teach us to remember You in the days of our youth. Forgive our many sins against You: our failure to thank You for undeserved blessings, our unspoken prayers, our failure to witness to the love of Christ, our words that dishonored Your name, our failure to avoid temptations. Remember not the sins of our youth, but remove them by Your gracious love in Christ, our Savior. Inscribe the image of Jesus on our hearts that we may remember His life and death for us. Deepen our faith in His love for us that we may respond with new life. Lead us by His love that we may remember His will in our home, at church, in school, at work, and in play. Your blessing we ask in confidence, through Jesus Christ, our Lord. Amen.

8

GRACIOUS GOD, because You have made us Your own by the victory of Jesus over evil, enable us to live out our lives for You. Help us to love as Jesus loved in giving His life for lost sinners. Open our eyes to the needs of others, and give us a concern for the welfare of the members of our family, our teachers and employers, our pastor and church leaders, all youth who struggle against You, the youth of our land, and all members of the body of Christ. Give us the courage of David, who faced Goliath without fear. Make us faithful, that like Joseph we may resist temptation and discharge all duties. In all activities of our life, lead us like Timothy to be examples in word and deed. Help us to value the precious gift of time as a call to Your service, through Jesus Christ, our Savior. Amen.

Youth Group
(Outdoor Meeting)

O BLESSED TRINITY, we lift up our eyes to the heavens that declare Your glory and see about us the proof of Your power, Your presence, and Your all-pervading wisdom. As we draw close to You, we sense more keenly how we have failed You and how much we need Your forgiveness and mercy. We therefore beg You to pardon our sins, to purify our thoughts, to promote good and wholesome desires within us. Help us dedicate the strength of our youth to Your service, and give us the grace to love You with dedicated affection. Bless our parents, our pastors and teachers, our counselors and advisers, and reward them for their understanding and interest in us. Give Your blessing to all the youth of our land that they may be brought to the Christian faith and join us in confessing and serving You, the one true and triune God forevermore. Amen.

Original Contributors

Julius Acker, Herman W. Bartels, G. Chr. Barth, Victor L. Behnken, Lorenz W. Blankenbuehler, Erich F. Brauer, C. F. Dankworth, D. D. Dautenhahn, L. J. Dierker, Walter E. Dorre, William H. Eifert, R. T. Eissfeldt, Herman A. Etzold, Erdman W. Frenk, Virtus Gloe, A. E. Going, Arthur W. Gross, Arnold H. Grumm, Roy E. Guelzow, Francis G. Gyle, Martin Haendschke, Emil C. F. Hartmann, Erwin H. Hartman, Wm. H. Hillmer, Martin H. Ilse Jr., Allan Hart Jahsmann, Richard A. Jesse, Alfred P. Klausler, Paul Koenig, Wm. A. Kramer, A. R. Kretzmann, J. P. Kretzmann, O. P. Kretzmann, John A. Leimer, A. H. A. Loeber, George A. Loose, Elmer E. Maschoff. R. H. C. Meyer, A. C. Mueller, Edgar J. Mundinger, Martin Neeb, Frederick Niedner, Rudolph Prange, Edwin Pieplow, R. C. Rein, Oswald Riess, Walter Riess, H. B. Roepe, E. J. Saleska, Roland H. A. Seboldt, Kenneth

R. Schueler, Roger L. Sommer, William von-Spreckelsen, Walter Stuenkel, Norman Temme, Clifford T. Voge, Martin Walker, A. G. Webbeking, T. A. Weinhold, Edwin L. Wilson, H. F. Wind, Elmer N. Witt, George W. Wittmer, and R. E. Wunderlich.